Essential Physical

SOLIDS, LIQUIDS AND GASES

Richard and Louise Spilsbury

Raintree is an imprint of Capstone Global Library Limited, a company incorporated in England and Wales having its registered office at 7 Pilgrim Street, London, EC4V 6LB – Registered company number: 6695582

www.raintreepublishers.co.uk
myorders@raintreepublishers.co.uk

Text © Capstone Global Library Limited 2014
First published in hardback in 2014
Paperback edition first published in 2015
The moral rights of the proprietor have been asserted.

Edited by Andrew Farrow and Abby Colich
Designed by Cynthia Akiyoshi
Original illustrations © Capstone Global Library Ltd 2014
Illustrated by HL Studios
Picture research by Tracy Cummins
Originated by Capstone Global Library Ltd
Printed in China by China Translation and Printing Services

ISBN 978-1-4062-5996-4 (hardback)
17 16 15 14 13
10 9 8 7 6 5 4 3 2 1

ISBN 978-1-4062-6006-9 (paperback)
18 17 16 15 14
10 9 8 7 6 5 4 3 2 1

British Library Cataloguing in Publication Data
Spilsbury, Louise.
  Solids, liquids, and gases. -- (Essential physical science)
  1. Matter--Properties--Juvenile literature.
  I. Title II. Series III. Spilsbury, Richard, 1963-
  530.4-dc23
  ISBN-13: 9781406259964

Acknowledgements
We would like to thank the following for permission to reproduce photographs: Alamy: p. 20 (© Nordicphotos); Capstone Library: pp. 14 (Karon Dubke), 15 (Karon Dubke), 28 (Karon Dubke), 29 (Karon Dubke), 40 (Karon Dubke), 41 (Karon Dubke); Corbis: pp. 9 (© Monalyn Gracia), 21 (© Alaska Stock); Getty Images: pp. 10 (the Agency Collection), 27 (Jeff Hunter), 31 (Travel Ink), 42 (ERIC FEFERBERG/ AFP); Nasa: p. 25 (Johnson Space Center); Nature Picture Library: p. 37 (Graham Eaton); Photo Researcher: 39 (Ted Kinsman/ Science Source); Shutterstock: pp. 4 (© tankist276), 5 (© BirDiGoL), 6 (© Kostia), 8 (© joyfull), 12 (© John A. Anderson), 13 (© Faraways), 16 (© beboy), 18 (© Olinchuk), 19 (© Denis Roger), 22 (© Alex Pix), 24 left (© Vit Kovalcik), 26 (© Vibrant Image Studio), 32 (© Four Oaks), 33 (© ckchiu), 35 (© Mikael Damkier), 36 (© Radu Razvan), 43 (© Ecelop); Superstock: p. 23 (National Geographic), 34 (PhotoAlto).

Cover photograph of sublimation of dry ice reproduced with permission from Photo Researchers (Matt Meadows / Science Source).

Every effort has been made to contact copyright holders of material reproduced in this book. Any omissions will be rectified in subsequent printings if notice is given to the publisher.

Contents

Eureka moment!

Learn about important discoveries that have brought about further knowledge and understanding.

DID YOU KNOW?

Discover fascinating facts about solids, liquids and gases.

WHAT'S NEXT?

Read about the latest research and advances in essential physical science.

Some words are shown in bold, **like this**. You can find out what they mean by looking in the glossary.

What are solids, liquids, and gases?

Look around you. All the things you can see and touch – your chair, this book, the water in your tap or glass – is **matter**. Matter is anything that takes up space. All matter can be sorted into groups. One way of sorting matter is into **solids**, **liquids**, and **gases**. For example, a brick is solid, water is liquid, and the air around us is a gas. All matter in our world, from the smallest speck of dust to the biggest whales in the sea, exist as one or a mixture of these three states.

We are made up of the three states of matter too!

The blood in our veins is liquid

The air in our lungs is a gas

Our bones are solid

If you look around again, you'll see lots of examples of the three states of matter in our world. The bricks, wood, and metal we use to build homes and furniture are solids. The milk we drink, the water we wash with, and the fuel we fill the tanks of our cars with are all liquids. Air contains **oxygen**, a gas we need to survive. We breathe in and out 15 to 25 times per minute, without even thinking about it, to get enough oxygen.

Eureka!

Englishman William James designed the first SCUBA gear (self-contained underwater breathing apparatus) in 1825. The diver wore a helmet and carried a supply of air in a metal belt around his waist and used this to breathe underwater for an hour.

Can you spot the solids, liquid, and gases in this picture?

Are all solids hard?

Many solids are hard or stiff, like wood or brick, but not all. Wool, clingfilm, and sponges are soft or bendy but they are solids too. A solid is something that has a definite shape. If you put a solid on a table, it keeps its shape and stays in one place. Solids also have a fixed **volume**. This means that they always take up the same amount of space.

DID YOU KNOW?

Diamonds are the hardest known natural solids. Some saws and cutting machines have tiny grains of diamonds along the edge to help them slice through metal, rock, and concrete.

Sand may spread out when we pour it from a bucket, but it is still a solid because each individual piece of sand keeps the same shape and volume.

Atoms and molecules

Atoms and **molecules** are the tiny parts or **particles** that make up all matter. Atoms are incredibly small – about 10,000,000 atoms could fit in a line across the full stop at the end of this sentence. They are often called the building blocks of matter. Just as a house is made of lots of small bricks, every substance in the world is made of millions of atoms. Molecules are made up of two or more atoms linked together.

Atoms and molecules are held together by pulling forces called **bonds**. Solids keep their shape because the bonds between their particles are very strong so they are held tightly together.

Eureka!

English chemist John Dalton (1766–1844) proved that all matter is made of atoms. He did experiments, worked out weights of some atoms and invented **symbols** for atoms and molecules.

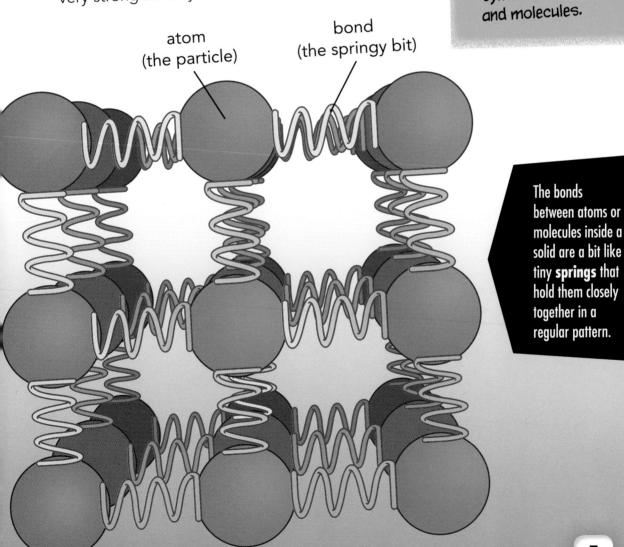

atom
(the particle)

bond
(the springy bit)

The bonds between atoms or molecules inside a solid are a bit like tiny **springs** that hold them closely together in a regular pattern.

How do we use solids?

We use different solids for different things because they have different **properties**. Steel and concrete have the property that they are difficult to break, even if you put heavy weights on them. This is because the bonds between their particles are very strong. So we use them to make bridges and buildings. Some solids, such as the metal copper, can be pulled and stretched easily, so we use it to make thin wires. Others, like wood, are useful because we can cut and shape them to make things like furniture.

WHAT'S NEXT?

Car makers are developing a new type of plastic for making solid car bodies. It is as strong as sheets of steel but 40 per cent lighter.

Giant skyscrapers have a steel skeleton, a frame of strong metal beams inside that supports the whole building.

Shaping solids

Some solids, such as clay and Plasticine, are useful because they can be pressed, shaped, and stretched into new shapes. Some solid materials are **elastic**. We can stretch or squash them out of shape, but they return to their original shape. Rubber and springs are elastic. If a solid is stretched too much, its bonds break.

▷

DID YOU KNOW?

When heated to the right **temperature**, shape-memory metals can be moulded into a shape that they never forget. They can be used in things like spectacles, so that if they get bent, the memory metal will soon go back to its correct shape.

When you land on a trampoline, you stretch the rubber and the metal springs. Both are elastic. As they return to their original shape, they pull back upwards and push you into the air.

Are all liquids runny?

All liquids are runny and cannot be held easily in your hands, but some are runnier than others. Some are thin and flow easily, while others are thick and gooey and pour more slowly. Thick honey and paint don't flow as quickly as milk or water, for example. Liquids don't have a definite shape like solids. They take the shape of the container you put them in. That's why they make a mess when you spill them on the floor – they spread out everywhere!

Eureka!

Scientists have been doing an experiment since 1927 to prove a thick black substance called pitch is the thickest liquid in the world. By 2011, just eight drops had fallen from the funnel of pitch they are watching!

Honey is a thick liquid so it can pile up for a short time before flowing into the shape of the container you put it in.

Inside liquids

In a liquid the atoms and molecules are closely packed together but the bonds that hold them together are not as tight as they are in a solid. The particles in a liquid can move around more, change places with each other, and spread out. That's why a liquid flows and doesn't hold its shape.

DID YOU KNOW?

Some insects can walk on water because of water's **surface tension**. At the surface of water, molecules hold on to each other more tightly. They form a thin invisible skin called surface tension.

The particles inside a liquid are packed quite closely together but they are not arranged in a regular pattern as they are in a solid.

container

uneven spacing between molecules

molecule

How do we use liquids?

As well as the liquids we drink, cook with and wash with, liquids have certain properties that make them very useful. Liquids have a fixed volume and they cannot be squashed. Think how firm a water balloon is when you fill it with water. This means we can use liquids to support things, such as water-filled beds and pillows that people sleep on.

DID YOU KNOW?

Living things are made up of 60–70 per cent water and need to drink water to replace that lost from body processes such as sweating and urination. Young people should drink at least 6–8 cups of water each day.

Some animals, such as sea slugs have spaces inside their body filled with water. They give the animal's body its shape.

Liquid power

When you push on one part of a liquid, that **pressure**, or pushing force, is carried to all other parts of it too. In **hydraulic** machines, such as diggers, pumps push oil through long, narrow pipes. This makes the liquid push on other parts that move the machine's digger arm to make it scoop and lift soil or rubble.

In many parts of the world people use water pressure to make electricity called **hydroelectric power**. Water flows down mountainsides and is forced through pipes that carry it through **turbines**. The water spins the blades of turbines to turn generators, which are machines that create electricity!

WHAT'S NEXT?

In 2011, 14 billion people did not have an electricity supply to their homes, to use for lighting, cooking, or heating. In future, small-scale hydropower systems might be able to supply many of these people with power.

This machine works using hydraulics.

Try this!

This simple experiment tests how runny a liquid is by seeing how fast something sinks through it.

Prediction

An object will take longer to sink in a stickier or thicker liquid than a runnier one.

Equipment

- stopwatch
- tall, thin glass with a line marked on the side
- steel ball bearing
- magnet
- paper towels
- liquids such as concentrated fruit juices, water, honey, clear shampoo, cooking oil, and others

What you do

1 Fill the glass to the line with one of the liquids and get your stopwatch ready.

2 Drop the bearing into the liquid without letting it splash. Time how long it takes for the bearing to sink to the bottom. Record the results.

3 Remove the bearing from the liquid by pressing the magnet to the outside of the cylinder and moving it upwards. Clean the bearing and repeat the drop two times.

4 Wash out the glass carefully using running water. Repeat steps 1–3 with the different liquids. Make sure you fill the cylinder to the same level each time to make it a fair test.

		Water	Honey
Time taken for a steel ball to sink through a liquid	1		
	2		
	3		

5 At the end, you should have a table that looks like this. Take the average time for each liquid and make a chart with your results.

Results
You should have found that the bearing sank quickest in water and juice and slowest in oil and shampoo.

Can solids become liquids?

If you hold a piece of chocolate or ice, it **melts** in your hands. Most solids become liquids when they are heated up. Particles in solids **vibrate** or move to and fro all the time, but they vibrate faster when heated up. These movements stretch and break some of the bonds between particles so they move around more instead of staying close together. The solid becomes a liquid.

DID YOU KNOW?

Chocolate melts at about 37°C (98.6°F), which is the same as your body temperature. That's why it melts in your mouth!

Different solids melt at different temperatures. These are known as their **melting points**. Ice melts at 0°C (32°F) but metals have very high melting points. This is because the bonds between metal atoms are stronger.

Magma erupting from a volcano is hot, liquid rock. When it cools in the air, magma becomes solid again.

Liquid to solid

To turn a liquid into a solid we cool it down. When a liquid cools, its particles slow down as they have less **energy**. The particles stay closer to each other and stronger bonds form between them. Gradually the liquid becomes a solid. We can change most substances from one state to another repeatedly by heating and cooling. For example, we can melt and **freeze** ice and water again and again. These changes are called **reversible changes**.

The temperature at which a liquid turns into a solid is called its **freezing point**.

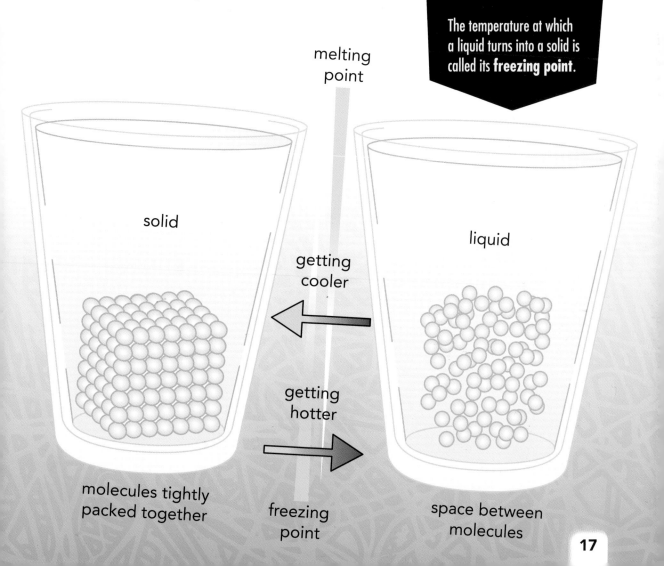

melting point

solid

liquid

getting cooler

getting hotter

molecules tightly packed together

freezing point

space between molecules

How do we use heating and cooling?

Many of the things we use are made by heating and cooling solids and liquids. Plastic is heated until it becomes liquid, then it is poured into moulds of many shapes, from spoons and plastic bottles to toys and chairs. When it cools and sets hard, it keeps the shape of the mould. When metal is hot and liquid it can be shaped and rolled into flat sheets used to make many things, from coins to computers.

WHAT'S NEXT?

Today, most plastics are made from oil but these cause **pollution** because they do not rot away. So scientists are working on new plastics made from plants that do rot away. There are already cups and plastic bags made from plants and many people predict there will be more plant plastics in future.

Thermometers work because the liquid inside them expands and rises up the tube when it gets hotter.

Bigger and smaller

Most materials **expand**, or get bigger, when heated and **contract**, or get smaller, when cooled. Solid things expand when they get hot because particles inside vibrate faster and take up more space. Solids contract when cooled because their particles vibrate more slowly and take up less space.

People need to allow for expansion or contraction when they make or build things. For example, road builders leave gaps in concrete so it can expand on hot days without cracking. People hang telephone wires loosely between telegraph poles so they don't snap when they contract on the coldest days.

DID YOU KNOW?

If you can't get a metal lid off a jar, ask an adult to hold it under hot water. Metal expands more than glass, so this will loosen the lid!

A steel bridge 100 metres (300 feet) long expands about 2 cm (1 inch) on a very hot day.

Can you mix solids and liquids?

Solids and liquids can mix with themselves and each other. A mixture is a jumble of different things, like when we mix up red, green, and yellow marbles. Many solids don't change when we mix them together, so we can separate them again.

A mixture of solids of different sizes can be separated with a **sieve**. The size of the holes in a sieve depends on the solids you want to separate. Gardeners use sieves to remove stones from soil. The holes are small to let bits of soil through but not stones.

DID YOU KNOW?

At a recycling plant, people use giant magnets to separate steel cans from aluminium cans. This is because steel is a metal that is attracted to magnets and aluminium is not.

Big gravel sieves like this are used to separate gravel from sand so it can be used to make concrete and roads.

When you mix some solids with water they stay separate, too. Some, such as cork, float on the water and others, such as coins or sand, sink to the bottom. We can separate some solids from liquids by sieving, like when we use a colander to drain pasta or peas. **Filters** are like sieves with very small holes to separate tiny solid pieces from liquids. Coffee filter paper has very small holes to let boiling water through but not coffee granules.

Eureka!

In 2006 Danish inventor Torben Vestergaard Frandsen created the Lifesaver straw. When you suck dirty water through it, filters remove dirt and chemicals kill germs to make the water safer to drink.

Holes in fishing nets must be small enough to catch fish but big enough to let young fish pass through, so they are able to grow to be adults.

How do solids disappear in water?

Some solids seem to disappear when you mix them with water! In fact, they have simply **dissolved**. They have broken up into pieces so small in the liquid that they can't be separated by filtering. This is what happens when we stir sugar in cocoa or salt in soup. The pieces of sugar and salt become too small for us to see, but we know they are still there because we can taste them. A liquid in which something has been dissolved is called a **solution**.

WHAT'S NEXT?

Scientists have developed protective plastic packaging for food that dissolves in water. In future we might be able to eat our sandwiches and the wrappers around them too!

Seawater is salty because it's a solution of dissolved salt in water. Most of the salt in seawater comes from tiny pieces of rock and soil washed by rivers and rain from land.

Sugar dissolves in water because the sugar breaks up into its individual molecules. These molecules spread evenly amongst the water molecules. Molecules are so small we cannot see them so the sugar seems to disappear.

We can make solids dissolve faster by mixing them with hot water. This increases the speed of the liquid particles, so they collide with the solid particles more often. Then the solid particles break free and are carried away more quickly. Stirring a solution also makes solids dissolve faster.

DID YOU KNOW?

Some liquids dissolve in other liquids, such as squash in water, but others do not. Oil doesn't mix with vinegar, it floats on top. That's why salad dressings often separate!

When there is an oil spill at sea, some oil floats and in calm waters can be skimmed or lifted from the surface, or even burned.

What are gases?

A gas is a type of matter that takes up space and has weight but it has no shape or size of its own. Like the air in the sky, gases can spread out in all directions and change their shape to fill any space.

Unlike solids and liquids, the volume of a gas is not fixed. It becomes the same as the container it is in. For example, when you blow air into an airbed, it spreads out to fill the gaps inside the bed.

Eureka!

Animals need oxygen to live. In 1772, Joseph Priestly proved that plants make the oxygen they need. He found that a mouse survived in an airtight box full of plants, but only lived for a short time in a box without them.

container

gas molecule

wide spaces between molecules

The molecules in a gas in this scuba tank are spread wide apart and they are always moving quickly in all directions.

If we can't see a gas like air, how do we know it's there? We know it's there because we can feel it. We feel air when the wind blows and we can feel it pushing on the inside of a balloon. This pushing force is called **air pressure**. We also know air is a form of matter because it weighs something. Try blowing up two balloons and hanging one from each end of a coat hanger so it is balanced. Then pierce one with a pin to let the air out and see what happens!

DID YOU KNOW?

Air pressure is constantly pushing all over us all the time, but we don't feel it. Air inside our bodies balances air pressure from outside!

There is no air and therefore no air pressure in space. Astronauts wear suits filled with air to push on their bodies. It stops their bodies puffing up and getting damaged!

How do we use gases?

We use gases in many ways. We burn natural gas in stoves to produce heat for cooking food or warming houses and helium gas is used to fill floating balloons. Carbon dioxide gas is used in fire extinguishers to help put out fires. It is also used to make the bubbles in fizzy drinks. We use air to fill things like rubber rings and tyres because air spreads out and pushes out from the inside of these things.

Helium is used in party balloons to keep them in the air. Helium gas floats because it's less dense than air.

DID YOU KNOW?

We smell things because air can carry tiny molecules of solids or liquids. This helps us smell pleasant things like flowers or perfume and warns us of danger - like when we smell smoke from a fire!

Under pressure

The big gaps between the molecules in gases also mean that gases can be **compressed**, or squashed, into smaller spaces. This creates a pushing force or pressure that can push other gases, liquids or even solids. For example, we compress air inside a bicycle pump when we move its handle up and down. This increases the air pressure inside the pump. This pressure then pushes air from the pump into the tyre to blow it up.

Divers use tanks of compressed air to breathe underwater. One tank of compressed air is equivalent to 300 of normal air!

WHAT'S NEXT?

Wind pressure can spin a turbine to make electricity, but it doesn't blow non-stop. In future some scientists think we could store compressed air in big bags on the seabed and release it through turbines when needed!

Try this!

Find out how much air is in your lungs! Blow through a straw into water and it makes bubbles. You can get an idea of how much air is in your lungs by capturing the air you blow out. One way is to blow into a water-filled bottle!

Prediction

The amount of water you can push from the bottle takes up the same volume as the air you blow out.

Equipment

- water
- 2-litre (3.5-pint) plastic bottle, with no lid
- washing-up bowl
- measuring jug
- about 1 metre (3 feet) of flexible plastic tube (new or clean)

What you do

1. Put water from a tap into the washing-up bowl until it is about 10 cm (4 inches) deep. Fill the bottle with 2 litres (3.5 pints) of water.

2. Put your hand over the opening of the bottle so no water can escape. Turn the bottle upside down and place the top of the bottle underwater in the bowl. Then remove your hand from the opening while holding the bottle still with the other hand. You could ask a friend to hold the bottle for you.

3 Now put one end of the plastic tube up into the water bottle and hold on tight to the other end.

4 Take a deep breath in so your lungs fill with air and then breathe steadily into the plastic tube until you run out of breath. You should see the water in the bottle fall in level and bubbling in the bowl.

5 Then remove the tube, put your hand over the mouth of the bottle, take it out of the bowl and turn it the right way up.

6 Use the measuring jug to fill the bottle back up. Record the volume you needed to add.

Results

When you blow air into the bottle, it displaces (pushes out) some of the water. You replaced the volume of water with the same volume of air from your lungs!

Can liquids become gases?

Liquids can become gases when they are heated. When a liquid gets hotter, molecules inside it move around faster and faster. This makes some of the bonds between the molecules break. These molecules escape from the liquid as gas. This is called **evaporation**. We see the effects of evaporation when water from wet washing **evaporates** into the air and dries our clothes or when puddles dry up in the sunshine. Evaporation is also what makes paint dry.

DID YOU KNOW?

In hot places such as Australia, people put covers over their pools when not in use to reduce evaporation and save water. Without a swimming pool cover, more than half the water in a pool can evaporate in one year!

When we heat water to boiling point, bubbles of gas form in the liquid, rise to the surface, and escape as **water vapour** (a gas) in the air!

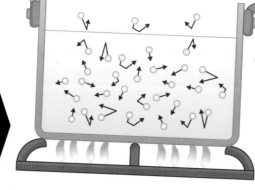

Cold water evaporates slowly as it turns into a gas and mixes with the air.

Water evaporates quickly when it is heated. When the water boils it turns into steam.

Evaporation happens at the surface of a liquid. That's why the speed at which a liquid evaporates depends not only on how hot the liquid is but also how large a surface area it has. So, a wide, shallow puddle dries up more quickly than a narrow deep puddle that contains the same volume of water. Wind helps things evaporate more quickly too, which is why washing dries faster outside on a windy day. The wind blows away the slowly-evaporating liquid molecules at the surface of the fabric. As they move away the next layer of liquid evaporates, and so on.

Clothes dry faster on hot windy days, especially if they are spread out and hung up high so more air can blow on them.

How do we use evaporation?

Our bodies use evaporation to keep cool. Sweat from your body is mostly water. When warm sweat evaporates from your skin and becomes a gas it takes some of the heat from your skin with it. That's why it is best to dry yourself quickly after a swim on a cold day, because evaporation of water from your body will make you even colder.

Eureka!

British inventor Emily Cummins was 21 when she invented a fridge for people who don't have electricity. It is made of two tubes, one inside the other, with wet sand between the tubes. When sunlight passes through holes in the outer tube and heats the wet sand, water evaporates and cools the inner tube, keeping its contents cool.

On hot days, elephants spray water on themselves with their trunks. Then they flap their large ears to speed up the evaporation process and help them to cool down!

Concentrate!

We also use evaporation to make drinks and food flavourings. Juice squeezed straight from fruit is mostly water, so people heat it and evaporate out the water to make concentrated juices. These keep for longer and are easier to store and transport because they take up less space. Concentrated juice can be **diluted** again, by adding water to it. In hot places, salty sea or lake water is left in shallow ponds to evaporate in the sun. The dry salt that is left behind is collected, cleaned, and crushed to make salt for people to add to food.

When water evaporates from these shallow pools of salty water, salt is left behind!

What is condensation?

Condensation is the opposite of evaporation. It is when a gas changes into a liquid. When a gas cools down, its molecules have less energy and move more slowly. Bonds start to form between the molecules. When the molecules join loosely together, the substance becomes a liquid.

We see the effects of condensation every day, like when water vapour from the air in a hot bathroom condenses into liquid on cold glass. It's these drops of water that steam up windows, mirrors, or shower doors!

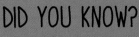

DID YOU KNOW?

You have to hold on carefully to a glass with ice in it! The outside of a cold glass gets wet and slippery when air around the glass cools down and makes some of the water vapour in the air condense into liquid on the glass.

Mirrors steam up when water drops condense on the surface.

Nuisance condensation

Condensation can be a nuisance. For example, it is the most common cause of dampness in buildings. When water vapour in warm air condenses onto surfaces in a home, such as wallpaper, the surface absorbs the water and moulds grow on this damp surface. They look unpleasant and can cause breathing problems.

Useful condensation

Condensation can be useful too. In places where water is in short supply, people evaporate dirty or salty water and then condense it. Condensation removes fresh, drinkable water leaving dirt and salt behind.

Planes leave contrails in the sky. Contrail is short for condensation trails, which are caused by condensation of water vapour behind high-flying jets.

What makes water special?

Water is special because it exists naturally in gas, liquid, and solid form: as water vapour in the air, liquid water, and ice. It is also unusual because it has more volume when it freezes – it gets bigger, whereas most liquids take up less space when they freeze into solids.

DID YOU KNOW?

Water is everywhere! Water covers 70 per cent of the Earth's surface, although most of this water (97 per cent) is salty and only 3 per cent is fresh. Of the fresh water, 85 per cent is frozen as ice mostly at the poles and on high mountains.

When rainwater gets into cracks in rocks and freezes, the ice expands and enlarges the cracks causing pieces of rock to break off!

Unusual ice

A kilogram of lead and a kilogram of feathers take up different amounts of space. We say they have different densities. Many substances on Earth shrink slightly and have greater **density** the colder they get. But when water freezes into ice it takes up about 9 per cent more space than it did as a liquid. Its density gets lower. That's why ice floats in your glass and why huge lumps of ice float as icebergs at sea.

WHAT'S NEXT?

Scientists know that Earth is getting warmer. **Global warming** is melting ice at the North and South Poles and increasing the level of water in our oceans. In future this will mean some coastlines are flooded and some islands are under water!

Ice floats, so only the surface of lakes like this freeze over. Living things at the bottom of the lake are still in liquid water, so they can survive the whole winter!

What is the water cycle?

The water cycle is the process of evaporation and condensation that recycles water on our planet. The sun heats up water on land, and in rivers, lakes, and seas, and turns it into water vapour. As this water vapour rises into the air, it gets cooler and condenses back into tiny drops of liquid water that form clouds. When water droplets become too heavy to float in the air, they fall as rain. Water runs over the land and collects in lakes, rivers, and seas, and the cycle begins again.

DID YOU KNOW?

The same water is used again and again so water you shower in today may once have flowed in the Amazon or been used to wash an ancient Egyptian's hands!

The world's water is recycled again and again in the water cycle.

precipitation

condensation

evaporation

river

lake

soil

ocean

Rain, snow, or hail?

Not all clouds make rain. On warm days a cloud may drift into a patch of warm air and the droplets of water that make up the cloud may evaporate. Clouds high above the ground are in very cold air and the water droplets inside these clouds form solid ice crystals. When these crystals bump together, they combine and become too heavy to float in the air so they fall from the sky. If the air they fall through is warm, ice crystals melt and fall as rain. If the air they fall through is cold, they fall as snow or hail.

Each snowflake is unique. No two snowflakes are exactly alike. Each one has ice crystals of different sizes and shapes.

Try this!

Water from vast oceans, rivers, and lakes evaporates into the air, condenses into mighty clouds and falls back to Earth over days and weeks. Demonstrate this cycle in a couple of hours on a warm day using a bowl, clingfilm, and a mug!

Prediction

Water from one place will move to another by evaporation and condensation.

Equipment

- large metal or plastic bowl
- large dry mug (or tall bowl)
- roll of clingfilm or a sheet of clear, flexible plastic
- small coin
- jug
- piece of string or large rubber band
- water

Method

1 Put the bowl in a sunny place outside.

2 Use the jug to pour water into the bowl until it is about quarter full.

3 Place the mug in the middle of the bowl, taking care not to let any water get into it.

4 Cover the top of the bowl tightly with the clingfilm. Tie the string or rubber band around the bowl to hold the film in place.

5 Weigh down the wrap over the mug using a small coin. Leave the bowl for 2 hours but watch what is happening inside. Now take off the film and look inside the mug.

Results

The Sun's energy evaporated water from the bowl and this formed a mist of tiny water droplets on the clingfilm above it. The clingfilm is a bit like the atmosphere because it traps water vapour. The droplets joined into bigger drops that moved to the lowest point of the film, where the coin weighted it down. The drops dripped into the mug, rather like rain.

Are all solids, liquids, and gases safe?

Many solids, liquids, and gases are useful and even vital for our lives. However, some are dangerous if not used carefully and it's important to know about these. For example, natural gas is perfectly safe when it is sealed inside pipes and used correctly. Natural gas leaks are rare, but dangerous because gas is **flammable**, which means it could catch fire if there's a flame or a spark nearby.

DID YOU KNOW?

The gas supplied to our homes doesn't actually have a smell, so energy providers add a smell of rotten eggs so people can sniff out a gas leak straight away!

Here a person is being evacuated after a gas explosion. Gas leaks are very unusual but if you do smell a strong gas odour, leave your home at once and do not use a telephone, turn any electrical switches on or off, or use a match or a torch.

Danger warnings

Gas has a smell to warn us of danger. Other hazardous solids, liquids, and gases have warning labels. Some have **symbols** that warn if substances are flammable or poisonous for example, or words such as danger, poison, caution, and warning. You should not touch medicines, bleach, and other cleaning products, or things you might find in a shed or garage, such as fertilizers, paint strippers, and thinners.

WHAT'S NEXT?

Soon there will be a set of international hazardous substance symbols that will be the same across the world. This will mean that anyone can spot a hazardous substance even if he is in a country where he doesn't speak the language.

Have you seen any of these warning symbols before?

Toxic substances are poisonous and could kill if swallowed.

Flammable materials catch fire and burn if exposed to a flame or spark.

Corrosive materials can burn people's skin and other things.

Glossary

atom everything is made up of tiny parts called atoms. Atoms are so small that we cannot see them.

bond force that attracts or pulls atoms and molecules together or towards each other

compressed squashed or pushed into a small space

condensation when a gas is cooled and turns into a liquid

contract decrease in size, get smaller

density how heavy something is for its size

dilute make a solution weaker by adding more liquid to it

dissolve when a solid seems to disappear into a liquid

elastic describes a material that returns to its original length or shape after being stretched or squashed

energy ability or power to do work

evaporate to change from a liquid into a gas

expand to spread out or get bigger

filter device like a sieve but with smaller holes that is used to remove solid particles from a liquid or gas passed through it

flammable describes something that catches fire easily and burns quickly

freeze when a liquid gets so cold it becomes solid

freezing point temperature at which a liquid turns into a solid when cooled

gas state of matter. Gases spread out easily because their atoms and molecules move around freely all the time and are not joined together

global warming increase in the temperature of Earth's atmosphere, probably caused by the burning of fossil fuels such as coal and oil

hydraulic machine that is operated by pushing a liquid such as oil or water through a pipe

hydroelectric power electrical energy produced by falling or flowing water

liquid state of matter. Liquids flow because their atoms and molecules are loosely bonded or joined together.

matter describes anything that takes up space and physically exists

melt when a solid is heated and becomes a liquid

melting point temperature at which a solid will melt

molecule group of atoms that are bonded or joined together

oxygen type of gas in the air that we need to breathe

pollution when dirty, harmful or dangerous substances are added to air, water or soil

pressure pushing force on a surface

property the property of an object describes how it looks, feels or acts

sieve mesh in a frame, used for straining solids from liquids or separating bigger and smaller solids

solid state of matter. In solids, atoms and molecules are held closely together in a regular pattern.

solution liquid in which something has been dissolved

spring tightly coiled metal wire that can be squashed or stretched out but that always returns to its original shape afterwards

surface tension force that strongly holds particles together at the surface of a liquid

symbol simple pictures, shapes, lines or letters that represent other things

temperature measure of how hot or cold something is

turbine machine that is powered by pressure from steam, water, or wind that is used in the generation of electricity

vibrate to move forwards and backwards or to and fro, quickly and repeatedly

volume amount of space that an object takes up

water vapour invisible gas in the air, water in its gaseous form

Find out more

Books

A Project Guide to Matter (Physical Science Projects for Kids), Claire O'Neal (Mitchell Lane Publishers, 2011)

Changing States: Solids, Liquids, and Gases (Do It Yourself), Will Hurd (Heinemann Library, 2009)

DK Pocket Eyewitness Rocks and Minerals (Dorling Kindersley, 2012)

Investigating Matter (Searchlight Books: How Does Energy Work?), Sally M. Walker (Lerner Classroom, 2011)

Life Cycles: River, Sean Callery (Kingfisher, 2013)

Solids, Liquids, and Gases Experiments Using Water, Air, Marbles, and More: One Hour or Less Science Experiments (Last-Minute Science Projects), Robert Gardner (Enslow Publishers, 2012)

Websites

teacher.scholastic.com/activities/studyjams/matter_states/
At this site you can watch video clips and do a quiz about states of matter.

www.bbc.co.uk/bitesize/ks2/science/materials/solids_liquids_gases/play/
On this BBC Bitesize site, you can play an interactive activity about solids, liquids, and gases.

www.harcourtschool.com/activity/states_of_matter/
Watch animations of molecules in solid, liquids, and gases.

www.thinktank.ac/featurespage.asp?section=907&sectionTitle=Solids%2C+Liquids+and+Gases
There is a choice of fun activities to do with solids, liquids, and gases at this website.

Places to visit

Visit the Sub Zero: The States of Matter room at The Liberty Science Center, Liberty State Park 222 Jersey City Boulevard Jersey City, NJ 07305, USA

Visit the Challenge of Materials gallery at in the Science Museum, South Kensington, London, SW7 2DD to explore many different materials.

See the effects of air pressure and more at the Science Mall in the Glasgow Science Museum, 50 Pacific Quay Glasgow, Scotland G51 1EA

At the Experimentations exhibition at The Powerhouse Museum at 500 Harris Street Ultimo, Haymarket, Sydney NSW 1238, Australia you can experiment with temperature and many other science ideas.

Further research

Some solids, like plastics and metals cans, are made from oil or rocks found below the ground. Find out more about how long it takes for plastic and aluminium to rot away or corrode and what you can do to reduce and recycle plastic and aluminium waste.

You could also find out about lava lamps. How and why do the blobs of liquid inside these lamps float in another liquid when warmed? Or you could discover the melting points of some different substances and find out how factories melt metals to extreme temperatures to be able to mould and shape them.

Index